A BRIDE IN THREE ACTS

By the Same Author

The Dance, The Cage and The Horse, Montréal: D Press, 1976.
A Queen Is Holding a Mummified Cat, Montréal: Guernica Editions, 1982.

A Bride in Three Acts
is the seventeenth volume
in the *Essential Poets* Series
published by Guernica Editions.

MARY MELFI

A BRIDE IN THREE ACTS

Guernica Editions

The Author and Publisher gratefully acknowledge financial assistance from the Canada Council.

Poems in this book have previously appeared in the following publications: *Exile, Northern Light, Descant, Montreal Poems, Prism International, Matrix, Mamashee, The New Quarterly, Germination, Ariel, Event, Prairie Fire, The Canadian Literary Review* and *Cross-Canada Writers' Quarterly*.

Guernica Editions, P.O. Box 633, Station N.D.G., Montréal, Québec, Canada H4A 3R1.

Typeset by Tanya Mars in Garamond No. 49.
Dépôt légal — 3e trimestre
Bibliothèque nationale du Québec & National Library of Canada.

Canadian Cataloguing in Publication Data
Melfi, Mary, 1951—
A bride in three acts
(Essential poets ; 17)
ISBN 0-919349-32-3 (bound). - ISBN 0-919349-33-1 (pbk.)
I. Title. II. Series.
PS8576.E46B75 1983 C811'.54 C83-090118-3
PR9199.3M44B75 1983

Contents

ACT ONE, SCENE ONE

ACT THREE, SCENE FOUR

La Demi-Vierge

It's your turn to be the blushing bride.
You don't blush (on cue)
but everything else runs on time
(including your parents' relief).

Who says you're a clog in a wheel?
Don't be so Victorian.

You're an inconspicuous hand grenade
    (with a life span of 'who knows?')
made to order for an inconspicuous/conspicuous
    computerized war (process).

God and the enemy are on holidays.

The groom takes over temporarily
but with an Arts degree
you don't trust his mechanical know-how
will change (exchange) your destiny.
(Was nuclear energy predestined (too)?
    You wonder. You worry.)

With the virgin insolence of a mechanical genius
you watch yourself tamper with the exploding
    population's equipment:
bodies: yours and his.

In due time no one is shocked to learn
    of your difficult(ies)
pregnancy: some peace treaty   (developed cheaply
    over the centuries).

A Man

The sun comes down one day
in the shape of a man with a radioactive cape.

He follows you.
Try what you might
you can't hide from him.
You can't hide underneath the shade of a tree,
    for one thing.
You can't hide in the basement of your bourgeois
    apartment building.
You can't hide at night:
he follows you to bed.

So you marry him.

The groom follows you to the bathroom.
You can't even be an animal and enjoy it anymore.

He stares at you and you think his stares are worse
    than bullets.
You won't know what hit you for years.

He means well, the poor bastard with the radioactive
   cape.
He's romantic. He's a heavyweight champion.
He loves you dearly.
After all, he did ask you to follow him till death
   do you part.
Following is so tragic.
You believe tragedy is the only ending suitable for a dull
   life.

Radioactivity, like romance:
in the beginning it makes things right; makes things
   grow; sex and all that.
In the end you're much too close for your own good.

Sometime afterwards the groom
follows you into your dreams,
more valuable than uranium.
He puts your dreams in an envelope
and seals it with a radioactive kiss.
Your dreams are radioactive.
No one will touch them with a ten-foot pole.

So you place his cape on your shoulders.
It's the only way to get out of the darkness.
   Ad nauseam.

On File

It's something like this:
you're only a part of something special,
and not the whole amount.
Analogy: you are a series of raindrops
(falling off somebody's hat to his/her annoyance),
but you are never the rain, answer to somebody's prayers.

It has always been like that, baby, since you can
    remember.
You always miss the boat.

Life is something like a movie with a lot of brides in it.
Then somebody edits the movie to make it commercial
and only one bride is left in it and it's not you.

Here you are happily married, with a bungalow,
and still you are a missing person

in the same way the good witch of the North
(Mom, a long time ago, colossal)
is now missing (on file).

Act Three

Paralyzed: you can't find spring entertaining.
It evaporates like some insignificant poison on your
    doorsteps.

You are caged by an intolerable sense of going nowhere
    special.

The rush of promises of a good life ends.
It's intolerable: your losses are piled up
on the heads of your kids like prize-winning books.

Winter warns you about something important
but you are lost in the barrens, reading a document,
annoyed by the fact you have to get up and make coffee.

You find your old dreams, orphans,
    dead in a refugee camp.
Despair tugs at your skirt, a naughty child,
    lovable at times.

You can't find the bride's old resentment against
    dying.
Ridiculed. You can't find the extravagance of the
    seasons, pretty.

You are less bridal than a songbird
less bridal than an electric saw
less in a hurry to be bridal
than spring is to be unsurprisingly majestic,
    surprisingly naive.

You can't find encouragement by loving the groom's
    inexhaustible smile.
You can't find your raison d'être in the groom's
    complaint about the nature of things.
You can't find the groom.
He's off punishing himself for not giving you
    a good life.

Failure is a motorcycle gang.
Gang raped, you carelessly look at yourself
    in a rearview mirror.
The metal frame around it is the world;
the rest is good-bye.

Struck numb by an obscene lack of hope, humor, faith,
your calendar looks like a sheet of ice
on which you will fall and break your neck.

Mercy Killing

The bride stores an old, somewhat primitive dream to be
especially, exceptionally rich and famous (oh great, so
  to speak),
next to an unappreciated wedding present: a vacuum
  cleaner. *Singer's.*

True to form, the vacuum cleaner,
follows the pattern of every science-fiction story.
It sucks up the bride's somewhat second-rate dream
  (like so many pins and needles).

In due time, the bride opens up the kitchen cupboard
and discovers the vacuum cleaner's constitution has
  changed.
It is beautiful. In the prime of its youth.

The housewife cleans up her life;
solo dances to the beat of cacophonic music
and comes to believe romance is kidstuff.

The groom is off exploring the universe; courageous,
but dead to all concerned.

The machine attends to the lady in question, daily;
somewhat satisfies her appetites to be ever so perfect.

The commoner's wife barely notices its mean
  (somehow, sexual) hold on her.
Her on/off days rush into the unknown.

Her old, somewhat second rate, primitive, vanilla-colored
  dream,
is hopelessly entangled in the machine. Nevermore.

Leaving Home

Failure trips you (the photojournalist) one day.
You turn around and try to take a picture.

The only reason you don't break you neck
is because the groom-to-be appears on the scene.

Mr. Nice Guy stops you from sleeping with men
    you don't like
stops you from eating too much junk food
stops you from misbehaving (against Mommy).

You marry Success.

One day Mr. Necessary doesn't live up to his reputation
(is reduced to a prop in a children's school play).

You, an amateur (Ms. Laughingstock) wrestle
failure by candlelight (no one's looking).

Rage

Rage, the bride whose dress is made of military badges
and whose groom is wearing deep scars,
will fight for justice for all — death being
the only ultimate justice she knows of.

Rage, the bride, with a bicycle chain around her neck,
says nothing about being a woman — soft as putty.
Her groom, despair, pays the price of her asexuality.

Rage curses, spits, hates injustice but is unjust.
Rage can make weapons look pretty, can make
hangmen's ropes and hangmen themselves look clean,
    spotless,
innocent — tools for righteousness.
Rage can sharpen a stone with her teeth
can use the stone to disfigure hope;
infect a child with hopelessness.
Rage makes flowers look like spots on a dress, dirt.

Rage once witnessed an automobile accident
and decided to set an automobile factory aflame the next
    day
(an eye for an eye, says the Old Testament).

Rage, the deformed woman, once visited the red light
    district
and sat down for a coffee with one of the prostitutes and
    convinced her
suicide was the only way out of the mess she was in.

Rage, the daughter of a woman whose intestines were
replaced by a mechanical device, is suspected
    of having pulled
the mechanical device apart
(because she had wanted to eliminate the disease
    from the face of the earth
but found she could do nothing at all).

Rage, the employee of death, rage nobody's friend,
rage, the employer employs vandals to destroy
    museum pieces.
Why bother to place art in some cage
    when most of the world is starving
particularly, when she's starving for something
    intangible?
Maybe love.

Rage is indifferent to calls for compassion,
calls for understanding, calls for respect to animal life,
indifferent to everything and everyone but her own
    dilemma:
how to make the authorities in hell understand the
    concept of justice
when hell is a prison for all that has been judged human
    and dirty.

Despair, the blackmailer, the rapist, the alcoholic,
    rapes her.
Rage screams in a barn where no one hears her
but the animals who take no note of her screams.
Rage, the bride whose womb was once used
    in a medical experiment,
rage, the antagonist, the protagonist, rage who wants
    everything
will be devirginized and pacified by the groom
    once and for all.

For *Children* Only

A grown woman skates across a bridge
to find the lost kingdom.

She only finds a woman who insists she is her mother,
who insists her house across highway 29 (across a
    cemetery)
is much too small for two grown women — if only she
    were a girl.

The lady finds herself a bachelor suite.
It fits her like her first pair of highheels. Baby shoes.
    Ouch.
She's claustrophobic and lonely. Constipated. Ouch.

She takes another business trip.
For a moment she thinks she is in hell.
The executives who make their living
out of 3-D maps and globes
map out her life for her. Made to order. Ouch.
She is lost. Annihilated like a bad sexual fantasy.

The woman takes a groom (to task).
She loves him like a suitcase packed with expensive gifts:
the only part of her journey (backwards through time)
which survived the ordeal.

The Best Friend

The bride walks down a hospital corridor.
Her loneliness is being operated on by the groom.

The bride's name tag says she's Ms. Suicide.
She believes her life has been reduced to an X-ray
    of her womb. It's ugly.

The calendar on her door was a valentine gift from the
    groom.
Some nut tore a page out of it, and wrote the word joy
    all over the month of June.

The mental patients are quarantined, or so it seems.
No one wants to visit them.

The bride's best friend arrives one day.
She places the bride's sickness in a bowl of sugar.

They drink tea together.
The bowl of sugar is a crystal ball.

The groom rollerskates down the aisle.
Someone's loneliness tap-dances on the operating table.

It's a musical. The patients are actors.
A set of twins in tutus braid the bride's hair.

With the lazy look of a cow or a victor
the bride walks out of the psychiatric hospital

and into a Japanese formal garden
on the arms of the director, the groom.

Her best friend takes a picture of them, with the
    hills beyond as background.
They're shaped like the initials of her name.

The Hypnotist

Hope is a woman with a gold watch chain,
swinging it right and left, left and right . . .
ordering everything to be under her control and to be
    dazzled by it.

So hope is a hypnotist
with the face of a woman who spent nights cramming
    for exams,
who was nearly ready to cheat on her medical exams
but said no to that sort of thing in the end,
and in the end did become a physician with a good
    practice in the suburbs
but gave it all up one day (as the story goes)
to become a hypnotist
(best new trick in town).
Since then she has been discriminated against by the
    rich and the poor.

But hope is a politician, a dictator, dictating hope
into people's lives on the weekend
(once organized a bingo game for the elderly and
    the sick).

Hope also drove across the country to see an eclipse of
    the sun
and took up mountain climbing in between.

Hope puts out her tongue to catch raindrops.
Hope confesses that she has a passion
for pistachio ice cream on a TV talk show.

Hope likes jazz on a starry night.
Hope plays the trumpet to recharge her batteries.

Hope also wants to be a millionairess and a mother
    of twins
by this time next year and at the same time maintain
    her reputation
and remain the one reason man cannot live by bread
    alone.

For the time being, hope is a bride, a midget,
who temporarily confronts rage with a smile.

The Match

Brides and grooms are labels for something: instincts.
Everyone, sometimes, challenges the purpose of an
   instinct in the twentieth century.

An instinct is a third person in a personal argument:
an observer to be loved and hated.

The instincts: love and hate, box each other.
The bride and groom watch.

In the old days a bride and groom would say hate was
   the devil himself.
Today they say it's only natural to hate (the xx/xy
   chromosome factor).

There's nothing to be done about it.
Hate isn't even mysterious (like the common cold).

The referee between love and hate isn't
a top ranking religious person (nor is it hellfire).

The referee between love and hate is
the instinct to think in the future tense.

The instinct to think in the future tense
makes the bride and groom careful when they fight.

To fight is as common as the U.S. drink, Coke, is
    in the West,
or as common as the impulse to ask forgiveness.

When the bride and groom fight they're as unpredictable
    as slot machines.
Except they run on guilt, and not on anything else.

Guilt is like an oil truck driven by an alcoholic driver.
Guilt is like a pair of glasses or a telescopic rifle.

Guilt is like a face of a clock (or of a mother, breast
    feeding).
It means nothing unless (the royal) we are in a hurry
    (to be loved all the time).

Love fits like a jewel but hate fits like a saw
which means hate isn't fitting, or logical.

The Dart Game

The bride puts up a picture of a once sacred man
  on her wall.
She draws circles around his head, not a nimbus, mind
  you, but circles.
                    Target practice.
The dart game has nothing to do with religion as such.
It is a symbol for all she once thought sacred
and which she had to abandon, lose,
in the process of aging in the twentieth century.

Till-death-do-you-part is a lost faith.

She is furious over the fact that she had to lose a
  cavalcade of illusions
just because she is clever and all that; a working girl.

The loss encloses her, the way a cage encloses any animal.
She is trapped in it. It won't permit her to walk out
of her loss the way she can walk out of a bathroom.

Often, she hits herself against the bars of the cage: loss.
If the bars were to be impaled into the very core of her
     being
she'd end up on a hospital table. She'd receive
     electric shocks
which would destroy a number of her brain cells
     (that's how the system works)
after which she'd function again. A dog trainer
     before and after.
Mercy killing in the reverse; she'd live on to tell her tale
of disillusionment at the divorce hearings.

Likely, the bride (who enjoys games and sports) will walk
     out of the cage,
out of her loss (one day) like an animal
walks out of a trap, with the trap on his foot — bleeding.
St. Jerome, the man who is supposed to remove the trap
     is dead
and so are his clone-like descendants.
More hunters in the twentieth century and so on than
     there are saints.

For while she misses her faith in till death-do-you-part
(a glass menagerie, a stable for the Christmas season
     only)
the loss helps her work harder to keep herself in good
     physical shape.
                    And young.

Familiarity Breeds Contempt

Marriage is a twin set of plates and cutlery
conveniently placed in the center of life

Marriage is a twin set of arguments (cagey & unnecessary)

Marriage is twin sets of boredom perched everywhere
    important

Marriage is a twin pair of orgasms
stranded on opposite ends of the spectrum

One woman declaring love blindly
One man declaring love blindly
to opposite ends of the spectrum

Two halves of something important: love and all that,
quartered day in and day out by truisms and the
    grotesque

Book II, Chapter I

"Happily-ever-after" is cut short.
The bride's and groom's "afterlife" is described in
   morbid detail.

Why
  a _____
  b _____
&c _____
is sinisterly better in (chosen) pairs

why
  a _____
  b _____
  c _____
&d _____
entertains / sustains (rarely disdains) his and hers

why
after a time always-the-same opulent disease:
love and aging boredom,
is a cut above lousy / louse's loneliness

and why
rigor mortis is seemingly content to take a longer
  time in coming to both
                             (bitterness)
                             once / just married [1]

[1]Footnote

ACT TWO,
SCENE ONE & TWO

Act Two

A small round desert: the wedding party.

Cigaret butts poke their heads into a hot hostile air.
  Bud.

Protagonists and antagonists both get a booby prize:
  smoke.

Free cigaret cartons on the table: decorations. Pop art.

How to welcome cancer with a smile?
Invite your boss to your wedding.
Smoke like the sexpot on the cigaret commercials.
Smile like a perennial (you're not).

An ashtray: a book somebody left behind.
New ones will be written by multinationals.

The bride owes her allegiance to a multinational.
When she's not a bride she's an IBM key puncher.

Her boss is a nasty chain smoker.

On Cue

Faces: cigaret butts.
Put them in a gun and shoot. Potluck.

Faces: smoke pointed towards the bride.
For fun: ''Why is someone always a hunter and
someone else always the hunted in the game of life?''

Blessed are those who heal the sick.
Doctor, help me.
I'm not happy like Noël at my sister's wedding.

So what?

At a masquerade everything is magical.
The mental health doctor can play the drunkard (he is)
    on his night off
and the patient can play the doctor
with the sterilized look of compassion (for free).

Smiles: cigaret ash, broken up on cue.

Words: ash and/or from dust to dust: remains of
    something not said.

The Tribe

The whole tribe is at the wedding.

It loves you for no reason.
The world is a global village: safe as a nutshell.

It's illogical:
you accept each member of the tribe into your heart
the way you always accepted obeying your mother as a
     kid.

Beware (you know): all membership rights terminate at
     the end of the party.
Blood relatives are as important to your life
as is a dollar to a spoiled kid.

Grandma's Missing

Her chair is occupied by a space.
The space is like a decayed tooth.

The space is like indigestion.
No meaning in life because your taste buds aren't in
    working order.

The space is like a donkey and other domestic animals
you'll never get to know on a friendly basis
because you are a city person.

The space is like a new highway built at the back of
    your house.
It clutters up your life with new noise.

The space is like an accident you see on the road.
You see the wreck and become afraid for yourself.

The space is like a friend who becomes a traitor.
You didn't think you had space in your life for a
    traitor, but you do.

The space is like a world war you were lucky enough
    to miss.
The space is like a world war anyway —
the space you leave open, afraid,
a war will fill up all the spaces in your life.

The space is like the continent of Africa.
You'll never see it because you're poor.

The space is a memory.
A memory is like a theatre the fire department says
    is a fire hazard.
It has to come down.

The Rose

The rose, prim and proper, a gift, on the table,
has something to say about the moment: the bride.
The rose, the smallest living item in the room,
says temporary beauty is enough if it's outside the
    human race.

The rose is ready to pounce on the bride.
Is ready to punch her in the face with its beauty.
It hurts; its color hurts her
because it is better than the color of her skin.

Sacred, that's it. The rose is sacred.

The rose, the focal point, the axis, the center of the
    world,
the savior, the foreshadowing of the messiah, the
    messiah,
the satellite fixed in space, watches, spies on the bride,
records her behavior towards her guests.
The rose is one of the eyes of God.

The rose tells its own story of creation;
a prehistoric backdrop, the heavenly rose: a stained-glass
    window.

The rose is a crystal ball
(serious and profound at its worst).
The bride wants the future she sees in it.
Serenity. Its ridiculous sense of serenity. Its extravagance.
She wants it. Damn it. She insists:
the rose is my slave; pitiless.

The rose is a key to escape.
The rose is an aphrodisiac.
Through it, because of it
the bride is inspired to forgive the world everything.

Turn off the light, thus thinks the bride,
let's pretend the rose is the light to see by.
In the light of the rose we are all brothers and
     sisters;
a family, familied by the rose. (Incest is OK.)

The rose is a head of a baby
which fell off to win more, better admiration: innocence.
The rose is a creature with a magnificent brain,
a brain whose dullness protects it against everything
     (n)everlasting.

The rose is at the head of the table.
It will never grow up, hurry and think:
rain is a series of insignificant miscarriages, godsent
(like the bride at/of the moment).

Gossip

Let's trade secrets.
Let's trade revelations.
It's a party.
How come the bride's so quiet tonight?

Silence is a textbook in any foreign tongue.
Conversation is a picture book. Go on.

Let's trade food for thought
whims
memories
stories
tragedies
violence repulses entertains scintillates accomplishes
    something.

Let's trade jokes
songs
ideas
sins
surprises
psychiatrists
restaurants.

Let's be patient with each other.
Delighted   ,,   ,,
Sarcastic   ,,   ,,
Wise   ,,   ,,
Compassionate   ,,   ,,

Exchange we-told-you-so glances.
Huddle close like ducks and ducklings.
Gain a feather in one's cap by exchanging Christian love.

Let's trade books, movies, performances in bed:
statistics: when, where and how? Good or bad?
Let's trade in our mechanical know-how to the bride.

Let's pour out our secrets like carbon monoxide.
Trade is what makes North America so great, old pal!

Words can infect or disinfect.
War with words: war dances.

Dance away fears, phobias, understatements.
Research says cancer is caused by
Research says cancer is accelerated by
Research says cancer is contagious
Watch out everybody will die one day like a guinea pig:
    abused.
Lily had a mastoidectomy. Gossip.

Be kind to individual week. To me. God. Please.

The bride will pick me up next week.
See you at her country place.
Be sure to bring your Ouija board.

On Strike

The bride can't get a hold of time
the way she can't take a pair of scissors and cut through
    the darkness;
a flashlight would do the trick
but the bride can't get a hold of time
the way she can't grab a pair of scissors and cut out her
    fear of the sea.
After all, time is more like the sea,
than a new road or downtown, dead or alive.

The bride would like to get a hold of time
the way she can catch a bus downtown on Saturday night
but she can't even take a small boat and cross a lake
so how can she hope to make time do tricks for her
    (e.g., standstill).

Time is on strike
(one strike against the employer of time),
because time wants more benefits out of life
than a silver platter or an Eaton's gift certificate.

The bride is in debt to time
but she can't pay her debts
because she can't get a hold of her greed.
It's always in the back of her like her spinal chord.

The bride can't get a hold of time
the way she can get a hold of a friend on a phone.
Time's line is always busy
(busily talking to her: hurry up or you'll miss the boat,
    Miss Monroe).

The bride can get a hold of time when she's sick though
but that doesn't count for much —
being sick is no way to pass the time.
Time is sick too;
sick of standing on balconies
and watching amateur actresses cruise bad parts of town,
    VD.

The bride eats.
The bride waltzes with dad.
The bride is happy as a lark
but she can't be happy as a lark forever
and the photographer and everybody else know it.

Time sings lullabies to retards.
Time is a war criminal preparing a cocktail.

Time is a bride who was late for her wedding
because she couldn't get a hold of her chauffeur.

Time after time someone named John is found dead on
    8th and Broadway.

When You're Hungry

Civilization can be reduced to a menu.

A book is for the dogs when you're hungry
but a menu brings out the best in you.

When brides eat with their guests
bread and butter come to life

and assure you that you are a touch better than the
   things you eat.

How to Learn to Forget Important Matters

A herd of sexual (*vs* celestial) beings are on the dance
    floor
stamping their feet to the beat of the music with the
    bride (Miss Jazz),
a parachutist who once won first prize at something
    important.

A herd of innocence is on the dance floor
stamping out all thoughts of death and destruction
(centuries of bloodshed taken off as easily as sets of
    dirty clothes).

Watch the herd (of colors) celebrate on the dance floor,
and you forget your ancient right to happiness is
    challenged (possibly) everyday.

The Bride: Your Employer

The bride opens the door and its handle becomes part
  of her hand.
You shake it.

A whole procession of ideas follows:
IBM typewriters, typewriters, type,
suicide by hard work, fast, faster, fastest.

The bride steals your identity.
Your salary depends on her blessing.

You want to leave the wedding (proof you are working).
You get tired (another proof you are working on the
  weekend).
You sweat (so you know you are at work).

Fairy tale, anonymous: a peasant's tears become skilled
  laborers overnight.
Fairy tale, twentieth century: union leaders drop out of
  nowhere and save

the oppressed. Except you haven't paid your union dues.

You are helpless.
The bride is ever present in your life like a phobia.
Like your impulse to disobey the Highway Code.

The priest at the wedding is an employer too.
Produce accordingly or you won't get a vacation leave.

The Gown

The bride's dress looks like a hospital gown.
You have a stomachache.

If you mentioned the fact
you'd be held responsible for the dull party.

The Ugly Guest 1

Her face is out of fashion.
It's made out of the wrong material.
It's patterned to look like something grotesque.

She is crippled by her birthright to have such a face.

It's a sign of weakness on her part to be ugly like that.
It's a sign her sex is virtually dead.

She is the antithesis of the bride.

If only she repatterned her face to fit the times.
If only a plastic surgeon could lay her hands on her.
If only.

You hate yourself.

You should know better.
You are educated.
You have no right to forget beauty is only skin deep.

So you rationalize.
There's something exceptional about her.
She could be a saint from the last century.

But she's shaped like a vacuum cleaner.
She sucks goodness out of you.

The Ugly Guest 2

His fame is his ugliness.
It makes you respect him.

You look at him the way you'd look
at a famous personality (in a coffin).

Still, there's something comical about him.
The man's a cartoon version of the Pieta.

His face inspires good women to be professional nuns
and bad women to be kind to furry animals.

His face comprises the face of an automobile accident
    victim
and the face responsible for the accident.

His face also makes you think of a sick child.
You'd like to protect it but you are as helpless
as when you witnessed the assassination of a great
    president on TV.

You can't do a bloody thing to help anyone miss hitting
    injustice.

The Mental Defective

Growing out of the mental defective's back: a cage of
   little monkeys.

The mob at the wedding is aghast by the little monkeys'
   lack of etiquette.
(At least Miss Edgar's and Miss Pimpernicle's pet
   monkeys were sensible; they stayed home.)

Can't ask the head waiter to throw the monkeys out,
   though.
The defective's mother is sharing the burden of shame.

Wouldn't it have been nice if the monkeys had come out
   of her womb —
out out like a good bowel movement — dead and
   dignified?
Wouldn't it have been nice if science had invented a way
   to kill off the monkeys and not the boy
like Vanquin kills off worms in one's guts?

But there is something human about the monkeys in the
   boy's cage.
Take a good look and men and women in wheelchairs, in
   cancer's grip,
schizophrenics, alcoholics, the dregs of society, appear
   out of nowhere.

Damn. It's not fair to the bride who's supposed to be
   crowned
with fertility tonight (and every other night).
May she not possess non-human (humorless)
   chromosomes. Of monkeys. Amen.

What is human? Ask a dog.
Excrement by another other (no)name is of human.
   Exactly.

The monkeys in the cage are dangerous.
They are poking out the eyes of justice.
Call the police.
Justice is defective.

The mob zero in on the bride's smile.
The monkeys' smiles, merciful like a heroine addict's
   needles,
zero in on the wedding cake.

All is quiet on the western front.

Wigs

Wedding guests feed you with safety.
They save you from being scalped by unpleasant news

(e.g., political animals can survive anything tragic).

Each guest is a page of an award-winning book.
The bride is the binding.

Each guest is a letter of the alphabet (and not any old
    number).
You have meaning only in relationship to each other
(nailpolish only means something to homo sapiens).

Hair falls off all the time
but a wig is important and should stay in place.

A wedding party is a wig on a collective head.

The End

The party's ended. And rosy cut rose
is relieved of its duty to be beautiful.

The party's ended: an astronaut's helmet, out of date.

To be relieved and frightened by one's fresh loneliness.
To be puzzled and delighted: one doesn't remember
    who were friends
and who enemies. Defenceless against such tactics as love
    and hate.

To be relieved and frightened by the turn of events.
One exposed one's secrets (like feces is exposd in a
    hospital lab).

Death is the ultimate excretion of all that is obsolete.
The whole body becomes an idiot's bowel movement.

Time to move on to another room with a better view:
sleep — a whitewashed toilet for partisan ghosts. Lazy.

The Wedding

7 dwarfs push wheelbarrows
filled with roses down a corridor,
a place full of Roman statues,
a museum, a mansion of a bride-to-be.

The dwarfs stop their wheelbarrows
in front of a boxing ring
and attach their roses to the boxing ring
(as if it were the brim of a lady's hat).

The guests enter.
The bride and groom enter.
The wrestlers enter. They beat each other.
The audience applauds.

The bride in her cumbersome white attire does not clap.
Her diamond rings impede her spontaneity.
Her groom is naked.
He sits besides her, a giant of a man. He yawns.

The wrestlers are replaced by a movie screen.
A film is shown.
The bride and groom exit.
Dwarfs of all shapes and colors follow them.

The Dwarfs

Snowhite delivers the dwarfs, her girlfriends (unmarried),
to an intensive care unit (or lonely hearts club).

Later, she discos with the groom in a mean cacti garden.

Later, the prince with some hesitation and difficulty
    transports the bride
(whose snowwhite-matching bra and panties were given
    to her by the dwarfs)
to a level of forgetfulness (or a new level of
    misunderstanding),
with the (un)decided help of a stag movie.

The dwarfs are transferred to a nursing home (a seaside
    resort, of sorts).
They play bridge and badminton (smelling like wedding
    bouquets).
The groom promised to introduce them to his two
    friends: doctor and dentist.

Later, Snowwhite complains to the dwarfs
who — wouldn't you know it? — (aren't burglars)
make up true confessions (compassion) for a living.

The dwarfs, her girlfriends (pill poppers) agree
happily-ever-after is lost on twentieth-century boys
who prefer to make paper airplanes out of Polaroid shots
   of nondescript virgins (to them: to romance).

Moral: a bride is only a door the groom makes sure
   to lock. Unlucky.
                    Good Nytol.

Out of Order

Period. The bride is out of order.
(Mother Nature is tidying up her affairs.)

The bride's smile will not win her anything (like it's
    supposed to).
E.g., her hotel room is dirty. Indifferent like a whore.

The bride is blue.
The blue bride is drunk with (machine) hormones.
    Hatred.
The groom is a cocoon of decay.

The sky is an easy chair the bride sits her dreams on.
Tomorrow, she will definitely buy herself something.

The Suitcase

A suitcase is like a honeymoon
and a honeymoon is like a flag of peace:
both promise to be passports to Exceptional Fun.

A suitcase is a royal we:
a potpourri of many strange things:
(boots and whips, for instance).

A bride is a space
and the groom is what often fills the blessed space:
a suitcase for kings and queens.

A suitcase is a sea of unknowns
a bride and groom swim in
until one of them gets cold feet.

A suitcase is someone running (with high heels).
Sometimes home is better — barefoot.

Home is what a bride and groom will travel
day and night to find in each other

(the way socks and pantyhose are often found
   in suitcases).

Bluebirds, Unimportant to a Comdemned Man

Bluebirds, unimportant
during traffic jams during fires during an A-bomb
    scare...

bluebirds lost in the masses the way an individual is
    lost in bad times

bluebirds pop out of the bride's honeyed dreams:
out of a book
out of the mouth of a policeman
out of his gun
out of a scream
out of a kiss on a movie screen (Charlie Brown's)
out of passion, compassion
out of everything bridal
constellations

out of three ads:
(No. 1) Drive the bluebird and you'll drive like a blue-
    bird: accident free;
(No. 2) Dial long distance (South) and you'll live
    through the winter loved like a bluebird;

(No. 3) Visit your municipal zoo and bluebirds
(flags of peace come to life, never soiled or poorly
   designed)
will watch you question the meaning of someone's yes to
   war and destruction...

Of   bluebirds   imitate
the   flight   of   the   rain
and   hum   a   potpourri   of   national   hymns
in the cartoon dreams of the cartoon-like, all in white, bride,
asleep   on   a   carton   of   political   events

Like One of His Birds

An employee numbered Too Slow is fired.
Sometime later he becomes a father
who wishes he were free as a bird (he isn't).

The manufacturer (of wooden birds) becomes rich.
He has his summer cottage built in the shape of a bird.

To help consummate his third marriage
the employer asks his young bride to dress up
    like one of his birds.

A&W

Boeing 747 decorates the bride.
The groom is part of her expensive outfit.

The passengers on the plane are only reflections
of her Christian mood.

Success is in the cockpit.
Play any game with the bride and she's the winner.

The bride anticipates her honeymoon by the strange blue
  sea
the way princesses (in pre-revolutionary times)
  anticipated coronations.

The bride is a potential target for creation.
She vows she won't be a waitress at A&W no more.

ACT ONE, SCENE ONE

The Transplant

A bride is like a mountain.
Empires rise and fall but she's unmoved by it all.

A bride is like a river.
She doesn't go out of date as fast
  as computer technology.

So the bride isn't a clock by any means.
You look at a clock to find out the time.
You look at the bride and think
a bride is more like a cow than a clock: friendly-like.

The bride is also someone you visit
when you are in a hurry to believe in romance.

The bride is a farmer who has to work in the morning.

The bride is an artificial organ
the twentieth century used in its open-heart surgery.

The bride is a defence against anxiety.
You look at her and forget
a war could do much wrong to you and yours.

The bride is a peace treaty
the twenty-first century may or may not throw into the
    waste basket.

The bride is a farmer who has to work in the morning.
Bread and butter taste good any time of the day.

The Picture

A motorcycle gang (trade name: Hell's Angels)
watch the purest of brides (in Parisian lace)
step out of a church.

The minister, an amateur photographer, takes a picture.

Down the Church Steps: a Divorcée

The bride accepts roses for a bad performance.
Nobody knows it was a bad performance except the critic
    nobody loves.

Nobody loves you either, dear, so somehow you feel
    forgotten:
deadwood, deadbeat, dead duck, dead — manikin-like.
But not like Pinocchio, mind you, who had a chance to
    be somebody.
You're a manikin invisible to the naked eye: humanoid
    and cold.

You look up at the sky and see an advertisement meant
    only for your eyes:
"You may fancy yourself successful but you're not.
You're only a puzzled failure whose life is falling
piece by piece all over the bride's dress (bird
    droppings)."

Nobody notices the bride's dress is soiled
like nobody notices birdshit on a highway anyway.
Somehow you also feel like a highway accident you once
    heard about on a radio.

Maybe all you need to come back to (terms with) life
is love in the shape of a dildo made in Taiwan.

Such a thing, guaranteed to last a lifetime,
is hidden behind the groom's wax smile. Didn't you
    know?
That's why the bride's gay and all-a-flutter today, like a
    ballerina, today.

You bet (underneath all that make-up) she's only rich
    and alive like a dead star
you don't know is dead because it shines in your face.

Somehow you take charge of your (better/bitter/biting)
    self
(someone you once knew successfully divorced it from
    marital bliss)
and run to get your car.

The poor thing's hungry;
looking forward to the wedding banquet
    (roast on the menu).

1:3

The wedding photographer's camera has a radioactive
  lens.
Click. Click. One won't see the scars left on one's body
  for years.

The bride's mother is crying her heart out.
She accidentally discovered a lump on her neck; could be
  anything.

The priest who married the couple won't go back to his
  office
and type up governmental forms (overdue) but he will go
  down
to purgatory and get a list of atrocities
the couple will suffer in the course of their lifetime.
If he is told they will be divorced (one out of three
  chances they will be)
then he will beat himself with a cane
because his special blessing will have been in vain.

Meanwhile a disturbed youth is going up and down the
  church steps.
He killed his father when he was five accidentally.
Now he is going up and down the stairs looking for his
  father.

The singer, the Ave-Maria man, tells his story to a guest.
He used to be an opera singer but old age interrupted his
    career.
The concentration camp number on his arm also tells of
    another story.

A psychiatrist, invited to attend his patient's wedding,
assures the couple he is willing to pump artificial life
into their marriage if it ever came to that;
the responsibilities of being married in the divorce
    capital of the world
might overwhelm his best customers.

One of the witnesses is an orderly, ready to use his
    ambulance
(parked illegally) to bring anyone to the hospital;
nothing is likely to happen. Everyone's gay.
The other witness is a divorce lawyer, the richest man at
    the party.

The wedding rings, everyone knows, are little computers,
    satellites,
where all the actions of the couple are recorded,
    conversations taped;
the rings are spies for the respective partners.
An accredited insurance company guarantees them for
    the life of the marriage.
However, once the couple take the rings off and pretend
they are not owned by their vows, divorce is in the
    offing; insurance annulled.

The fans cheer the couple who run and jump over
    obstacles.
Temptation to move on to another bride or groom
(another bride or groom being like another profession)
is one of the greatest obstacles in their path;
a great sports event for all comers.

An ex-mechanic set up an appointment with the
    (self-lacerated) priest,
allowing the priest to believe the car was a bride-to-be.
The priest's anger on discovering the deception is
    mitigated
because an angel steps out of the car, pats the priest's
    head, and assures him a church is a garage.
Men and women come there to get themselves a good
    fix.

Life goes on for one out of three (elsewhere).

Some Spinster Believes

A groom is better than a winning lottery ticket because
    the prize money
is alive. A groom is better than unemployment
    insurance.
A groom is not nearly as wonderful as an astronaut on
    the moon
but much more ready at hand (to do the dishes).
A groom can be picturesque, at times.
A groom is like a fan, a fan made of guarantees:
sex twice a week on hot nights.
A groom is not like an old bridge,
but a spinster with heart disease is. Isn't she dumb?

A Beautiful Woman

A beautiful woman is a wedding album.
Here comes the bride all over again.

She is the woman on a tapestry,
sometimes with a child on her lap as decoration,
    sometimes embroidery.
Her maids do all the labor for her.

Simultaneously, she is the best virgin of the century,
(when virgins are in demand)
and the best sex symbol of the century (when sex is in
    greater demand).

She is always the promise of a fresh beginning,
the water you wash your face with after a disturbing
    dream;
the well, desperate men draw their dreams from.

She is a folk song, a classical piece, rock-and-roll, jazz.
She is a feast, the horn of plenty, a menu for
    connoisseurs.

She is whatever you like most in life.
She is Miss Whatever-she-wants-to-be.
She wins the first prize: a trip to identity.

Her beauty is a book which ranks with a Ph.D. thesis
on the behavior of the atom.
Her beauty is an introductory course
at a junior college on the psychology of the aborigines.

She is knowledge of the best kind: nature is kind.
You look at her and are appeased by nature's cruel jokes.

For she is never sick.
When she tells you she is sick you don't believe her.
She is energy.
The woman who turns on the ignition key.

She is a surprise party.
She makes you forget about routines, appointments,
    forget to hurry,
forget about corruptions in governments, bureaucracy,
    old age.
She is an international lady,
a diplomat from some unrecognized heaven of sorts.

She sells you cars, perfumes, hair dyes, shoes, trips to
    nowhere special (on TV),
and you like her a lot.
She is a saleswoman, selling faith, hope and charity.
    Credible.

She sells you brides' clothes. On sale. Half-price.
She sells you promises: marry the beauty and the beast
and all will be well with the world. Halleluja.

The Sermon

The bride is something like a typewriter
the priest writes a sermon on.

The priest reads his sermon through a microphone.
The microphone being like a groom.

The sermon reminds the congregation
that marriage isn't part of a film rehearsal.

There's something cold and metallic about marriage.
It has to be metallic to last through sickness and all that.

It's a magician's job (sort of) to see to it
the metal and the sacred consummate properly.

The Striptease

Someone drums up the courage to do a striptease.
She reveals in the process she is a dancer (of sorts).

Spring is a stained-glass window.
The sun an ESP orchestra.

Here comes the groom, fresh out of college,
and athletic like the stripteaser's first husband.

The marriage ceremony commences on an optimistic
    note.

The minister is the hope for a brighter future.
The witness: history repeats itself.

B-Flat Major

Just because the paid singer is doing his job alright
(while the bride's signing herself off to the unknown)
you'd think simple birds could carry great destinies
in their beaks in lieu of worms (question marks on the
    meaning of life).

Just because the paid singer is paying a compliment to
    the moment
you'd think musical instruments were stranded
    in mid-air
and statues of the church's patron saint will come to life.

It's not a moment to make light of though.
You'd never think, for example, Miss Cinderella
    will rush out of the blue
(whereupon more cartoon characters would follow suit)
and pay tribute to the bride (or the children, if they
    behave): instant royalty.

The future's an unknown soldier, sometimes.

It's a solemn moment.
All other moments are like candy in comparison: no
    good for you.
You'd think leaders of enemy forces were signing peace
    treaties.
Everyone is so solemn.

You'd think the bride and groom were a new bridge,
    worth millions of dollars.
Or a first prize everyone won with a great deal of effort.

The paid singer makes sure now is not the time
to be too ambitious, or to catalogue failures in a book,
or remember a near suicide who became a millionaire
out of desperation for a meaning in life.
Now is not the time to think about what to buy
    at the supermarket,
or the high price of beef. Or the time to get
    down to basics:
what year did Armstrong discover the moon anyway?

For sure it's not the time
you'd expect a man in a wheelchair, bitter,
    to insist on his right
to walk away, untouched by the blushing bride
    (by Yardley Enterprises).

It's a happy happier-than-thou blueless moment. Jazz.

The paid singer's simple *Ave Maria* in B-Flat Major
is a rocket and the bride is the engine of the rocket.
She engineers the trip out of town, to outerspace.
Her veil is made of fibre optics.

Along the way guests are shown time-lapse films
    of flowers ablooming
and women, bared ass, all abloom too. No siree.
    Porn's out.
Now is the time to be civilized.
Pull the wool over one's eyes.

The paid singer's musical vowels and consonants
are a cushion for all of life's mistakes. Sexless.

You'd think the bride weighed down
    by the magical moment would cry. She does.
You think for a moment
    (like the fool you are for high-class romance)
birds will come and make a water fountain
    of her lament. They don't.

I Remember

Grandma,
the princess,
Grandma,
an empire of acceptance,
Grandma,
an empire of better best mothers
(like spotted dogs, dolls, bingo: adorable).
Grandma, the harlequin,
Grandma, the trampolin, I jumped on
    when Mother wasn't looking,
Grandma, the fireplace,
Grandma, the lady with the mouth of a lion,
    a playground,
Grandma, my protectress,
Grandma, the lady in waiting who introduced me
    to the queen: myself,
Grandma, who obeyed her vows (to baby)
    like a dear dear dear,
Grandma is worn out. Worn out like a nineteenth-century
    idiom. Dead. A heroine.

Grandma, my heroine, your coffin was just a suitcase
    with nothing in it.

I see you hiding behind the altar, behind
the pews, behind great grandsons' smiles,
while this (that) bride promises away everything
     to a groom. Peekaboo.
Love-and-death is only a peekaboo game.

Pallbearer No. 1 turns on a tape recorder
and Grandma's rich coffee-bean voice startles the world.
Pallbearer No. 2 projects a film on
     Pallbearer No. 3's back:
a screen of clearest Grandmamma memories.

Pallbearer No. 4 flips through the pages
     of a photo album
where Grandma and I are star figures.
Pallbearer No. 5 holds an umbrella over his head
to make sure I remember Grandma saved me
     many a time.
Pallbearer No. 6 holds a candy jar on his head.
Grandma, the candy store; I remember.

Grandma, the lady on the mount who fed me
(I was her multitude of worries, her multitude to feed)
Grandma, who turned a loaf of bread into a full course
    meal,
Grandma, the nightclub singer, and I
    the drunk at the bar,
Grandma, the peasant woman,
who couldn't read, who couldn't travel,
who couldn't do anything because she loved me,
Grandma, who didn't train me to be an adult,
who packed the toilet trainers off to work and left
    me with her
(like a wall is left with another wall,
two equals holding a big house: important),
Grandma, the surprise,
who didn't surprise me with report cards or postcards,
Grandma, who'd hand me pieces of the good life
Mother forgot to bring home after work,
Grandma, the woman who gave me a lovely sense
    of myself and Italian history,
Grandma, the woman who made sure this (that) bride
would not be missing on earth,
Grandma, I remember.

Hello Ms. Love-object, first and most important.
Welcome to the wedding.

I Do

Your face, sinless like watercolors

Your face like a cloud
Your face like all clean things

Your face which I won't exchange for a bar of gold
Your face which I won't deface with a bar of gold

Your face like a church's pew: useful
Your face like a church's ritual answers to ritual
    questions
Your face like an assembly of churchgoers, united,
    to praise something

Your face, common perhaps, but male and mine

Your face untainted by deadly unknowns
Your face incongruous in a domestic crowd
    of apprehensions: poverty

Your face, I know it. I know your face.

Your face is a stop sign.
It stops me from entering a country where
there would be no liberty to be what I gracelessly am.

Grateful that your face delivers grace,
grateful that your face delivers kisses
like signed petitions are delivered to good
     and bad governments

Your face helps me get into life's good graces

Because your own face has a singular grace about it
     like a great country,
has an exceptional grace like that country's museums,
has unprecedented authority like that country's supreme
     court of law,
your face helps me believe in the revolutionary slogan,
justice for everyone, here and now, (please)

Your face poses itself like a no
Your face negates all my attempts to say no to love
Your face knows what I know
and can say no to me, and yes to me
because it knows how to pose like a no

You look at me
like a water fountain:
health pours out of your mouth

Your words are like water: useful, better than water:
    addictive

With your eyes, ears, mouth like
with your eyes, ears, with a mouth like firecrackers:
    surprises
with your eyes, ears, with a mouth like blades of grass:
    harmless

With your smile for my eyes, ears, mouth
with your smile for our excursions into arguments

With your smile for our excursions
when we wrap ourselves with flags of peace
and unwrap ourselves of bourgeois excuses
not to consummate id/ego/superego's marriage vows
        once again

I can swear my cup runneth over with Yes
for all faces, posed yes or no to my own face,

my own face, at times, lost, in your face
like wrinkle, scar, birthmark

Act One

The smile is a cathedral,
renovated to fit the twentieth century.
The smile is an acrobat,
ready to please the twentieth century: awkward sneer.
The smile is a giant octopus in an aquarium,
indifferent to the smiles of school children.
The smile is a Japanese formal garden.
The smile is a fortress.
The smile is a toddler in the arms of an old person.
The smile is a galaxy of brides.
The smile is a world fair
seen through the eyes of a prisoner on parole.
The smile is a symbol for all that is right with the world.
The smile is the best of all possible habitats
    earned by hard work.

The smile, a pastoral setting.
The smile, the Milky Way on a dull photograph.
The smile, an oxygen tank.
The smile, the beauty and the beast after falling in love.
The smile, a lottery ticket.
The smile, the prize and the new standard of living.
The smile, a fistful of sunlight and a fistful of hope,
    hocus-pocus.

Smiles, the cornerstone of civilization.
Smiles, the lace tablecloth, expensive, on an old table.
Smiles, archangels dancing on the head of a safety pin:
    the earth.
Smiles, envelopes enveloping good things.
Smiles, cargo boats.
Smiles, a bucket full of exclamation marks and commas.
Smiles, the translation of an archaic language: English.
Smiles, a picture book, a diary of better dreams.

Smiles the bride and the cathedral; the groom
    and the office building.
Guests smile. Radio news, TV news, newspapers smile
and say nothing at all. Thank heaven.
The sky smiles, helped by a kite.
The sun smiles without any help.
The wind's smile is contagious like a drummer boy's.
The rapids rapidly smiled on a coureur de bois and his
    canoe some time ago.
The heat smiles and the potato harvest
    takes a while to smile back
but it smiles back in due time.

The smile resembles a woman cleansed of all mean
   thoughts.
The smile resembles the shape of vaginas and penises:
vertical and horizontal at the same time: shapes without
   boundaries.
South East North West all smiling at the same time.
The smile resembles a duet.
The smile resembles a man wild and hungry
   to hurt no one.
The smile cuts out hunger, anxiety, anger, hatred, greed
   (temporarily).
The smile cuts down one's ridiculous perception
   of a ridiculous world.
The smiles hunts down death wishes and dumps them
   off the Arctic coast: ice food.
The smile is out to rediscover the meaning of life.
The smile is out to make one forget the meaning of life.

The smile is nutritious.
The smile advertises life everlasting. Ho ho ho.

The smile insists on an honest bride and groom
who need not smile in bad times.
An honest smile is a blessing, the second shower
of the day
(before words come and change everything
for better or worse).
An honest smile makes atomic waste
look like the mess in one's bedroom closet.

To smile is not simply a challenge, but an instinct.
To smile is to decorate one's life
with the search for happiness.
To smile is to give civilization its obligatory dowry.

One smiles like a cat licks its tail;
it makes for a good pet.